DRUMSET INSTRUCTION

IN THE POCKET

Grooves and Fills Based on Latin Clave Patterns

**Applicable to Rock, Funk & Other
Contemporary Styles**

by JOHN SNIDER, JR.

CD INCLUDED

ISBN 0-634-09253-7

HAL•LEONARD®
CORPORATION
7777 W. BLUEMOUND RD. P.O. BOX 13819 MILWAUKEE, WI 53213

In Australia Contact:
Hal Leonard Australia Pty. Ltd.
4 Lentara Court
Cheltenham, Victoria, 3192 Australia
Email: ausadmin@halleonard.com

Visit Hal Leonard Online at
www.halleonard.com

Foreword

"John Snider's new book *In The Pocket* is a book that every serious drummer should have in their library! I love the concept of applying clave to rock, funk, and other contemporary styles. I have always had a very strong feeling that drummers of all ages need to constantly be improving their stylistic knowledge, and *In The Pocket* will help YOU to achieve this goal!!!"... Gregg Bissonette

ABOUT THE AUTHOR

John Snider, Jr., originally from Bakersfield, CA, is a drummer, clinician, and teacher who lives and works in Miami, FL. He spent 12 years providing the infectious groove for Eddie Money, touring, recording, and appearing on the *Tonight Show*, *Late Night*, *Regis and Kelly*, *Rosie O'Donnel*, *VH1 Top 20 Countdown*, Carl's Jr. and Rally's commercials, and the list goes on. He can be heard on Eddie's *Right Here* and *Unplug It In* CDs as well as the *Shakin' with the Money Man* CD and DVD. He also did the *Fall in Love Again* video that appeared on VH1. Other credits include *New Frontier* on Columbia Records, *AKA Lance* on Empire Records, Tully Winfield, *Burning Candles* with Tommy Girvin, and back in the early days the Kern Philharmonic, Jazz Philharmonic Quartet, and the Bakersfield Civic Light Opera.

THANKS FOR YOUR SUPPORT

John Good, Don Lombardi, Garrison, Scott Donnell, and everyone at D.W. Roy Burns, Chris Brady at Aquarian, Rich Mangicaro at Paiste, and everyone at Vic Firth.

SPECIAL THANKS

Everyone at Hal Leonard, Ed Roscetti—I can't thank him enough, Gregg Bissonette and family, Ron Castonguay—tagging the name "In the Pocket," Mark and Neil Moralez and family, Eddie Money, Bob and Theresa LeBarre, Tommy Girvin, Randy Forrester, Lee Beverly, Bobby Levine, Chris Frazier, Brian (Wookie) Wolk, Jeff Weirick, Jon Graves, Frank and Tully Rosato, Don Schiff and family, Lance Muggleston, Joe Porcaro, Maria Martinez, Melissa Castonguay, and Trent Stroh for his amazing playing on the CD.

VERY SPECIAL THANKS

My incredible and amazing wife Diane and our son Stormy; my sisters Roberta and Darline and the whole gang; the McElfresh family; and my mom and dad, Lillian and John, Sr., whom I miss very much.

EQUIPMENT

John endorses D.W. drums and hardware, Paiste cymbals, Aquarian drum heads, and Vic Firth sticks.

DEDICATION

This book is dedicated to our son Stormy. He has taught us that miracles do happen.

CREDITS

Drums and Percussion: John Snider, Jr.
Additional Percussion: Ed Roscetti
Bass: Trent Stroh
Keyboard-bass and Pre-Production: Jorge Silvestrini
Drum Tech/Cartage: Cory Flanigan
CD Mastering: Damon Tedesco

All songs composed and arranged by John Snider, Trent Stroh, and Ed Roscetti, Groovetoons (ASCAP), Trent Stroh Music (BMI) © 2004 All Rights Reserved.

CD produced, recorded, edited, and mixed by Ed Roscetti at Roscetti Music, Studio City, California.

Table of Contents

Page

Introduction. 4

Chapter 1: Clave Patterns 5
   Patterns. 5
   Up and Down Stroke Technique 6
   Accenting on the Clave. 7
   Ride Ostinatos 8

Chapter 2: Grooves and Fills 9
   Bombo. 9
   Son 11
   Rumba 12
   Bossa Nova 14
   Samba 15
   Afro Cuban 17

Chapter 3: Groove and Fill Combinations 19
   Various Grooves 19
   Splashing the Hi-Hat 32
   Quick Reference Guide 34

Chapter 4: Playing the Charts. 36
   Bambo. 37
   Son 38
   Rumba 39
   Bossa 40
   Afro Cuban 41
   Samba. 42
   Alternative Clave. 44

CD TRACKS

Track

Chart 1 Bombo with drums   1
Chart 1 Bombo without drums   2
Chart 2 Son with drums   3
Chart 2 Son without drums   4
Chart 3 Rumba with drums   5
Chart 3 Rumba without drums   6
Chart 4 Bossa with drums   7
Chart 4 Bossa without drums   8
Chart 5 Afro Cuban with drums   9
Chart 5 Afro Cuban without drums   10
Chart 6 Samba with drums   11
Chart 6 Samba without drums   12
Chart 7 Alternative clave #3 with drums   13
Chart 7 Alternative clave #3 without drums   14

Introduction

This book came about through noticing that a lot of hit songs I've learned through the years were based on Latin clave patterns. Songs such as Sting's "If I Ever Lose My Faith in You," Eddie Money's "Trinidad," and Journey's "Can't Tame the Lion" are all based on 3-2 son clave. The clave gives you a foundation to create an endless source of rhythm. If you think in clave, you'll never be at a loss for rhythmic ideas. Because of this, I started writing out patterns for my students. I put the clave mainly on the bass drum and added the ride and back beat patterns. To their amazement, they were groovin' —that's what it's all about. Once you hear yourself lay down that groove, you're hooked, and the journey begins. I hope this book either continues or begins your journey into an endless amount of enjoyment and accomplishment.

HOW TO USE THIS BOOK

I recommend that you get comfortable playing the clave pattern with your feet first. This will make it much easier when you're ready to add the hands. After you master one of the patterns, turn to pages 6 and 7 and begin putting the accent patterns with the clave pattern in your feet. When playing the ride ostinatos, play on an x-hat or ride cymbal at first so you can develop playing the hi-hat with your foot. The grooves are presented on the left side and fills on the right to make it easier to choose a fill while you're playing the groove. Play an eight-bar phrase—either seven bars of groove and a one-bar fill, or three bars of groove, two beats of groove and two beats of fill, followed by three bars of groove and one bar of fill. Play the first eight measures on the hi-hat, the second eight on the ride cymbal, and repeat. The groove and fill should be played with the metronome for two or three minutes, as if you're playing a song, before stopping. After you've mastered a few grooves and fills, try playing one of seven charts corresponding to the grooves you've mastered. You don't have to wait to master everything before playing the tracks. Pick what you're into for that day.

ABOUT THE CHARTS

There are seven play-along tracks with corresponding charts. The chord changes have been included, so I recommend getting together with other musicians to play the charts. This will really help work on your time feel. Use the grooves and fills in the book, and from those examples, you'll start to get the idea and be able to create your own. Also, the charts are in order, one through seven, so you can easily pick through and choose the chart of the day. Have fun, groove, and play "in the pocket."

NOTATION KEY

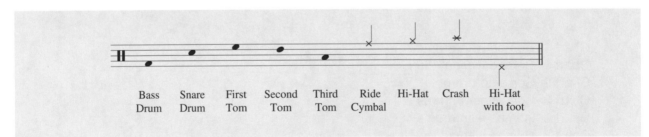

| Bass Drum | Snare Drum | First Tom | Second Tom | Third Tom | Ride Cymbal | Hi-Hat | Crash | Hi-Hat with foot |

Chapter 1: CLAVE PATTERNS

PATTERNS

On the left-hand column is the traditional rhythm. On the right-hand column is the rhythm applied to the bass drum, with the hi-hat playing eighth notes with the foot. I have included three additional rhythms that I call *alternative claves* **A**, **B**, and **C**. These rhythms are used often for the foundations of songs.

1 Bombo Clave

2 Son Clave

3 Rumba Clave

4 Bossa Nova Clave

5 Samba Clave

6 Afro Cuban Clave

7 Alternative Claves

A.

B.

C.

UP AND DOWN STROKE TECHNIQUE

- The *down stroke* (D) is your accented stroke. It starts with the tips of the sticks pointing up at about a 75 degree angle. Strike the drum and pull in your second (middle) finger slightly and stop the stroke about an inch above the drum.

- The *up stroke* (U) is your soft stroke. It starts about an inch above the drum. Relax your wrist; let the tip of your stick hit the drum. Then, your elbow should move slightly away from your body as you lift your forearm back to the down stroke starting position.

- The *tap stroke* (T): start about four to five inches above the drum. Strike the drum and return.

- The *full stroke* (F): start at a 75 to 80 degree angle above the drum. Strike the drum and return.

Play the following exercises using the strokes mentioned above:

Sixteenth Note Patterns

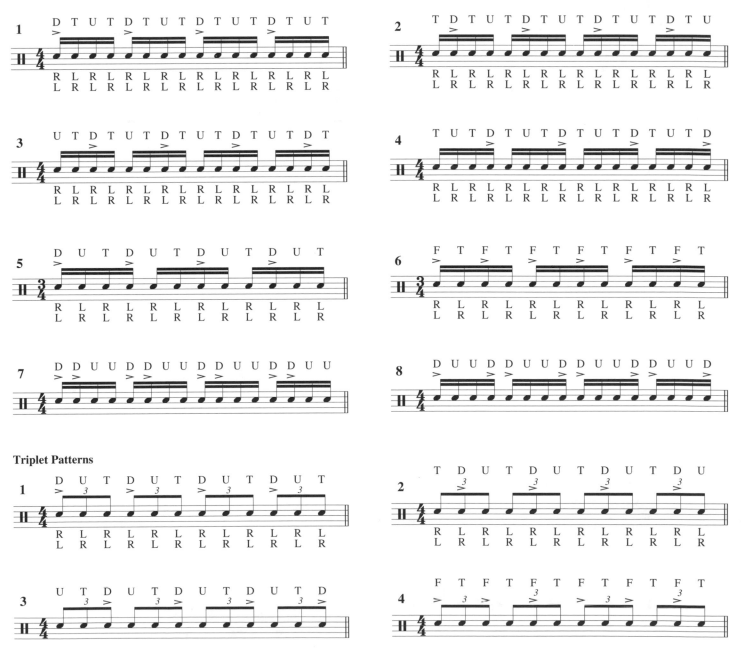

Triplet Patterns

ACCENTING ON THE CLAVE

The accented notes correspond to the patterns on page 5.

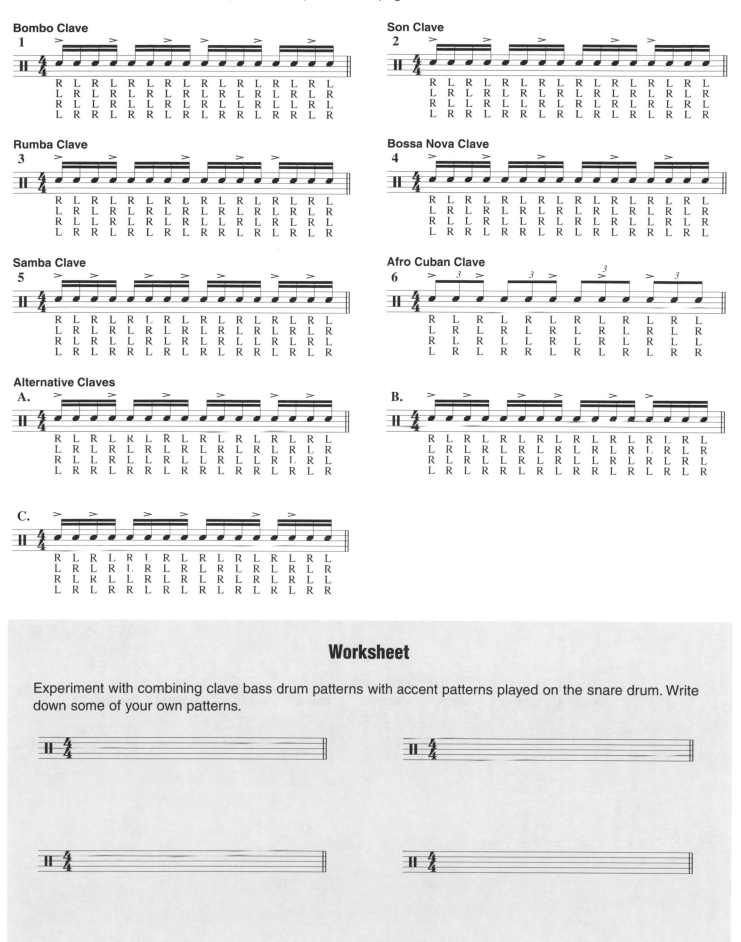

RIDE OSTINATOS

These five ride ostinatos are to be applied to the clave bass drum patterns on page 5. Play beats 1 and 3 on the bass drum only, until the up and down stroke technique on the hi-hat becomes comfortable. Note that your speed and dynamics will determine the height of your sticks from the drum or cymbal. The instructions on page 6 for the up and down stroke are only a starting point for the technique.

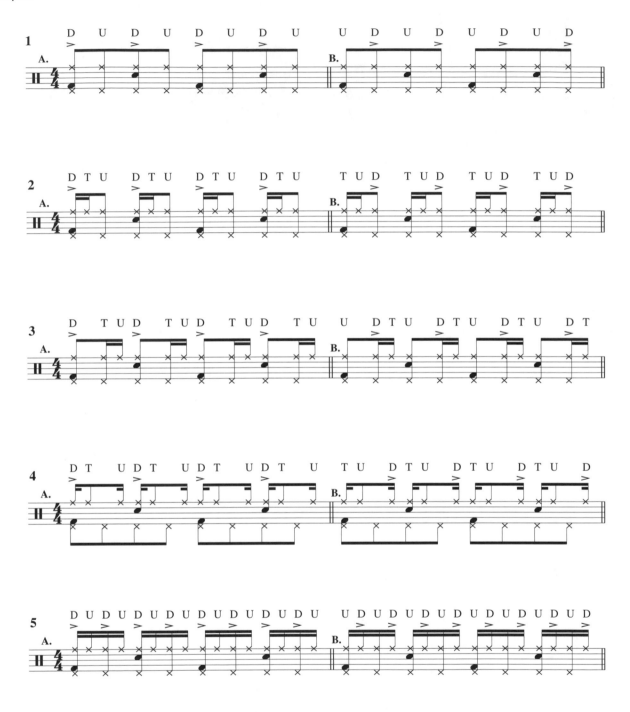

Chapter 2:
GROOVES AND FILLS

BOMBO

BOMBO GROOVES

Get comfortable with the grooves and fills in the straight feel. Repeat each one with the swing feel. Also, play in an eight-bar phrase—seven bars of groove, plus a one-bar fill.

BOMBO FILLS

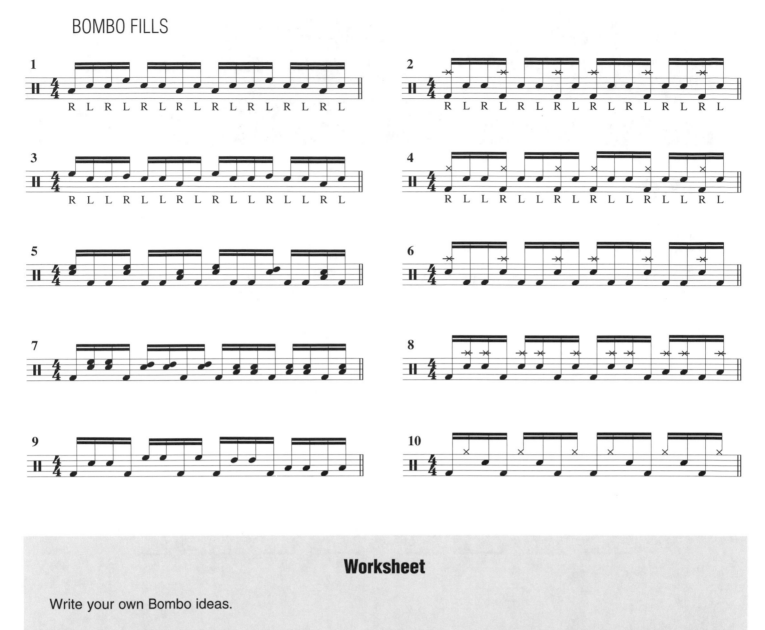

Worksheet

Write your own Bombo ideas.

On the grooves, try adding the bass drum on the "and" of beat 1 or leave out the bass drum on the "and" of 2—experiment.

On the fills, create your own. You'll get the idea from the exercises. Remember to think in clave!

SON

THE SON WITH OSTINATOS 1 THRU 5

Play the exercises with both a straight and a swing feel.

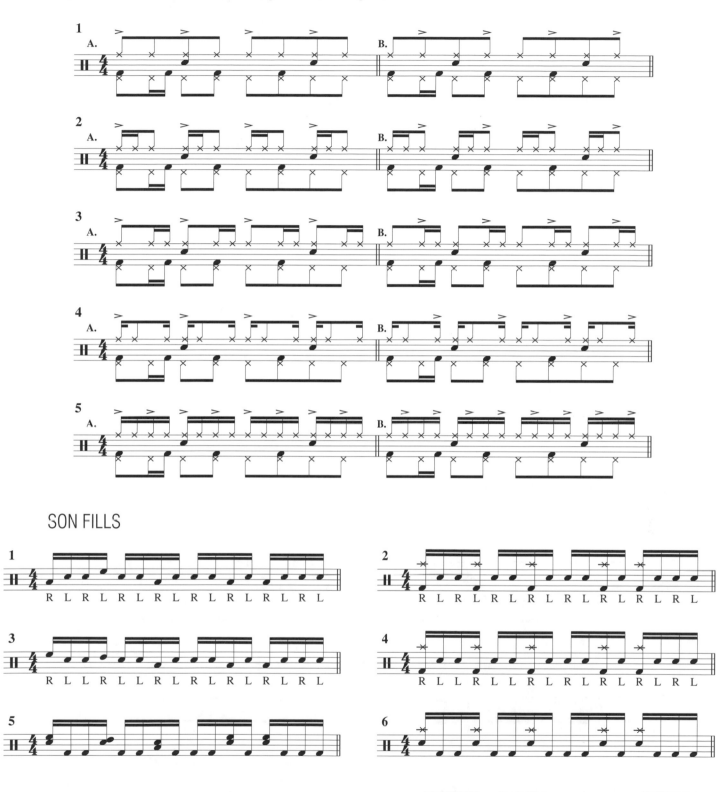

SON FILLS

Worksheet

Create your own.

RUMBA

THE RUMBA WITH OSTINATOS 1 THRU 5

RUMBA FILLS

Worksheet

Remember, the orchestrations that I wrote are not in stone. Write out your own orchestrations for the fills.

BOSSA NOVA

THE BOSSA NOVA WITH OSTINATOS 1 THRU 5

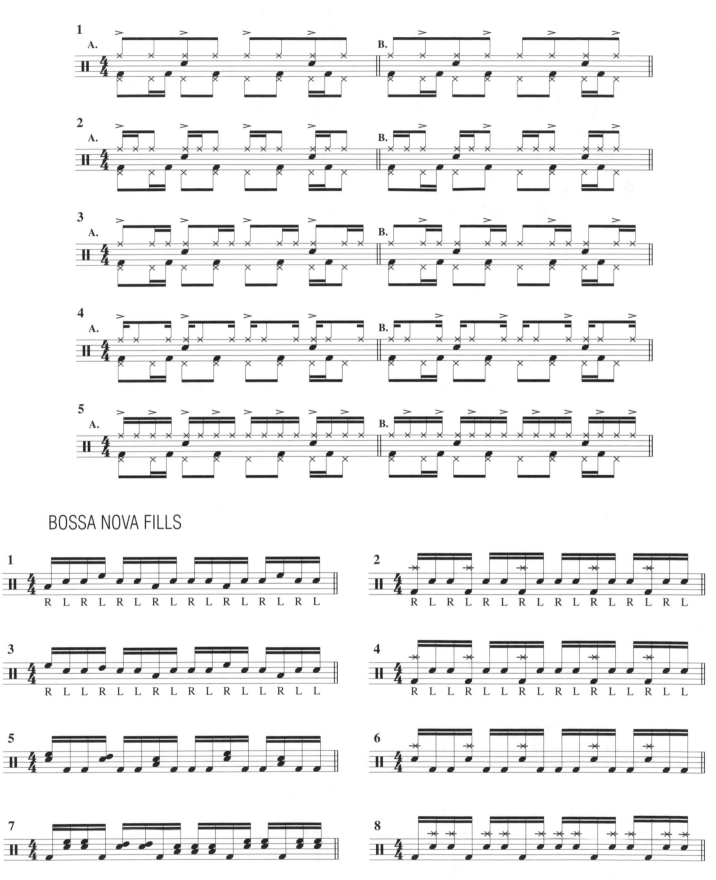

BOSSA NOVA FILLS

Worksheet

Try playing six bars of groove and two bars of fill. When playing the fill, play the first bar on drums only. In the second bar, play the accents on the cymbals with the drums in between. Have fun and experiment.

SAMBA

THE SAMBA WITH OSTINATOS 1 THRU 5

SAMBA FILLS

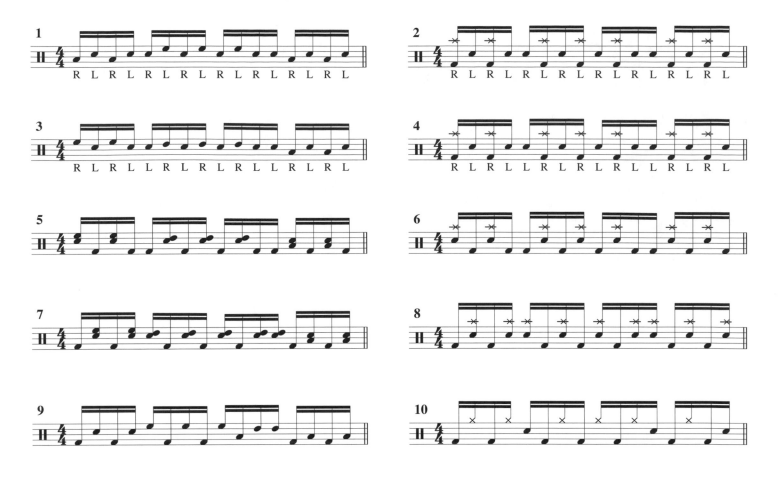

Worksheet

Remember, experiment with adding and/or leaving out bass drum beats.

AFRO CUBAN

AFRO CUBAN GROOVES

Afro Cuban with the shuffle ostinato, including ghost-note variations, and half-time feel.

(♩) = ghost note—a note played only faintly, for effect.

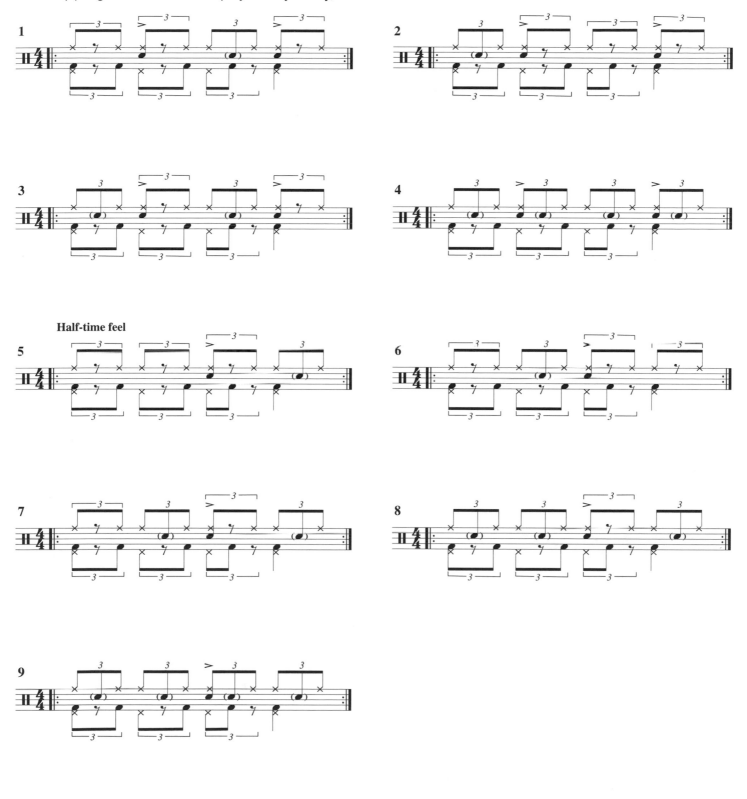

AFRO CUBAN FILLS

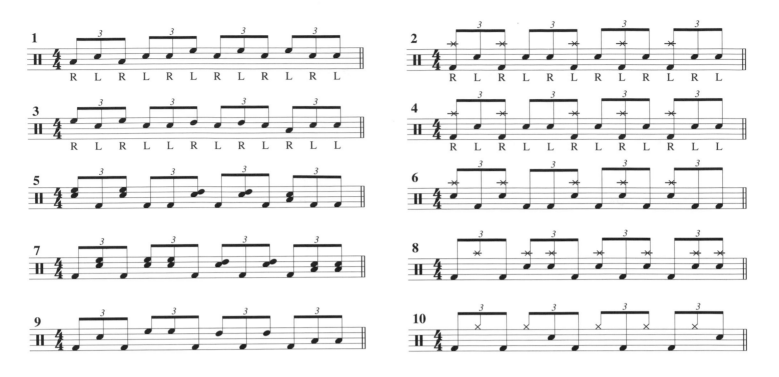

Worksheet

Work on different phrasing:
2 bars groove—2 bars fill
4 bars groove—4 bars fill
6 bars groove—2 bars fill
8 bars groove—8 bars fill

Also, mix the fill patterns while doing the phrasing.

Chapter 3:
GROOVE AND FILL COMBINATIONS

The following grooves and fills are based on all nine claves that you practiced on page 5. They are in a random order, with ostinato number 1 and nine ghost note variations. You will notice by going through these exercises with straight and swing feels that these grooves fit in a variety of different styles—rock, funk, hip-hop, jazz, and ethnic music. The clave pattern gives you a foundation from which to create. *It's not just for Latin music.* Where would we be if we didn't have the clave patterns? The following hit songs would not exist: "Rosanna" by Toto, "Fool in the Rain" by Led Zeppelin, "Late in the Evening" by Paul Simon, and of course, all of Bo Diddley's hits. The clave pattern serves as the foundation for an endless list of hit songs.

VARIOUS GROOVES

VARIOUS GROOVES WITH OSTINATO #1 AND NINE GHOST-NOTE VARIATIONS

Play these with the metronome at different tempos.

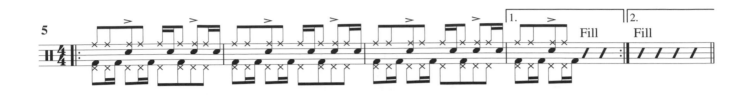

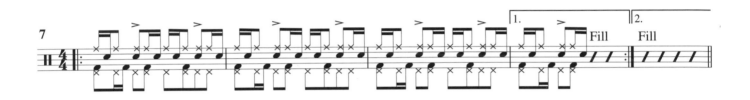

FILLS ON THE CLAVE

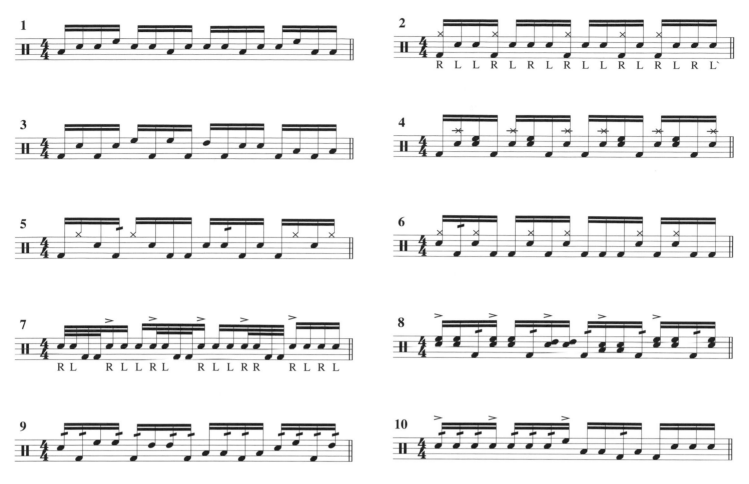

Worksheet

Try writing your own fills with any clave. Put the accents on the toms and the rest of the strokes on the snare. This should get you started.

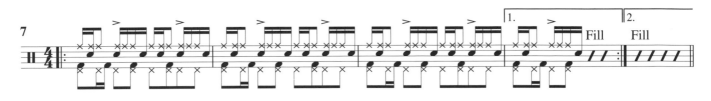

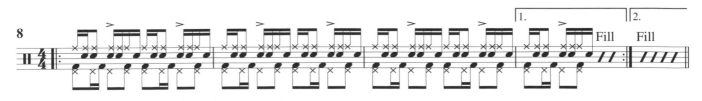

FILLS ON THE CLAVE

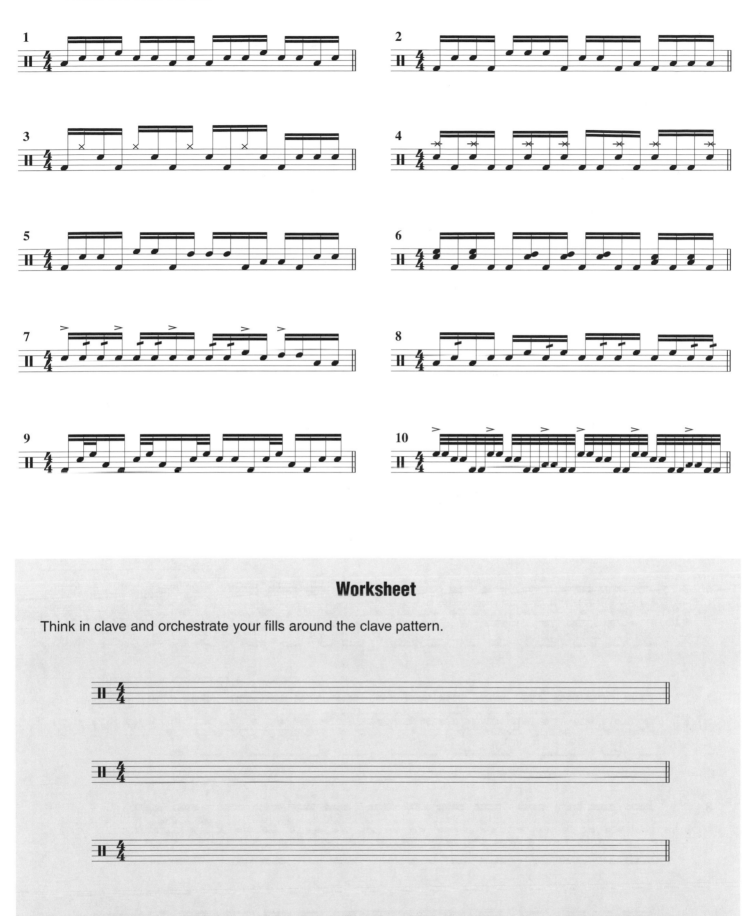

Worksheet

Think in clave and orchestrate your fills around the clave pattern.

CLAVE GROOVES WITH OSTINATO #3 AND NINE GHOST-NOTE VARIATIONS

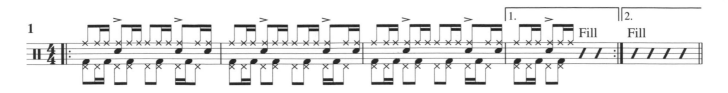

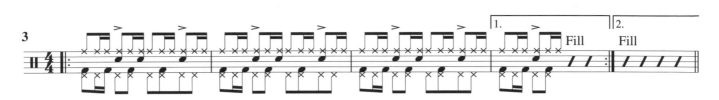

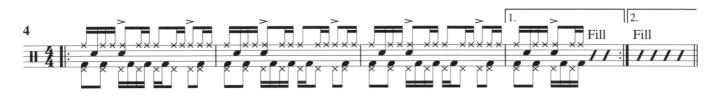

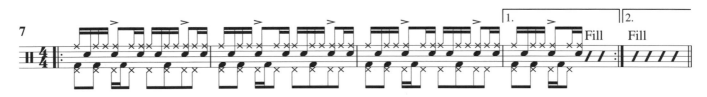

FILLS ON THE CLAVE

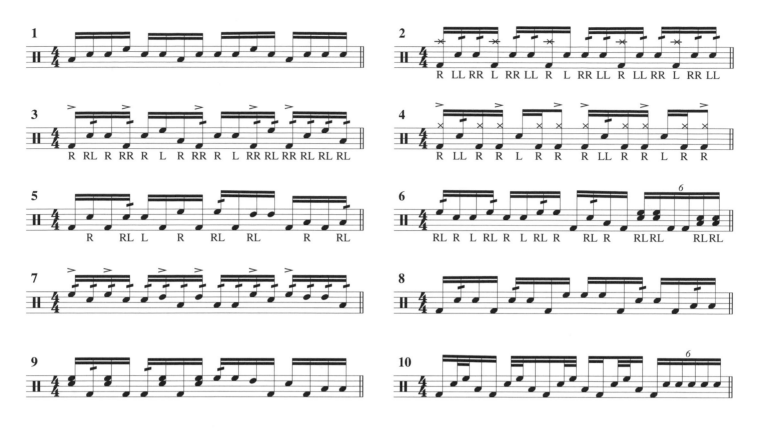

Worksheet

Create your own fills based on the following:
1. Play sixteenth notes with single strokes—accents on the toms—non accents on the snare.
2. Play sixteenth notes: Right hand on all the accents, hitting toms or cymbals—left hand in between on the snare.
3. Play sixteenth notes: Bass drum on all accents—hands play together in between—left hand on the snare—right hand on the toms or cymbals.
4. Play sixteenth notes—bass drum on all accents—hands play single strokes in between.
5. Play sixteenth notes—hands play together on accents—left hand on the snare—right hand on toms or cymbals, bass drum plays in between.

CLAVE GROOVES WITH OSTINATO #4 AND NINE GHOST-NOTE VARIATIONS

1

2

3
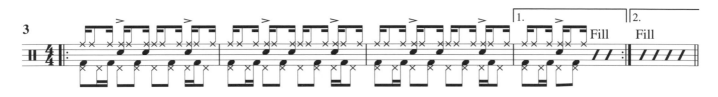

4

5

6
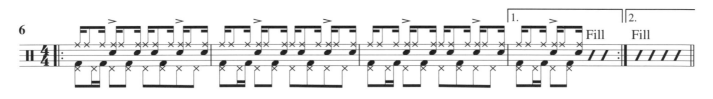

7
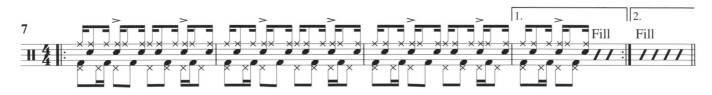

8

9
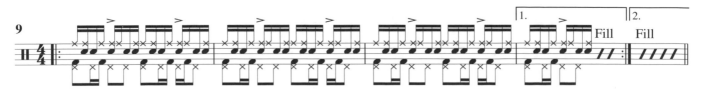

FILLS ON THE CLAVE

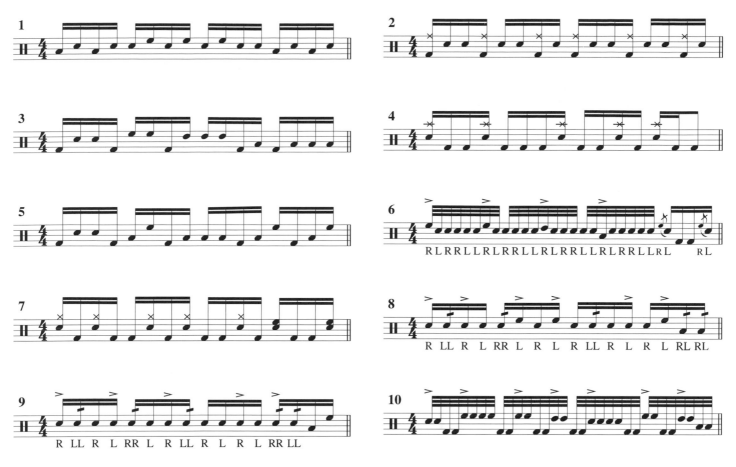

Worksheet

By now you've gone through the ride ostinatos. Next, try your hand at mixing the ride patterns with your favorite bass drum pattern.

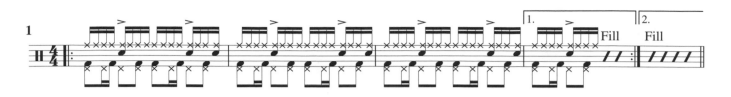

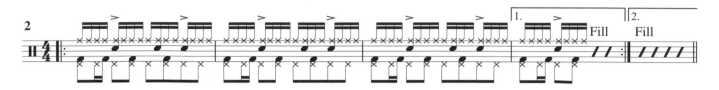

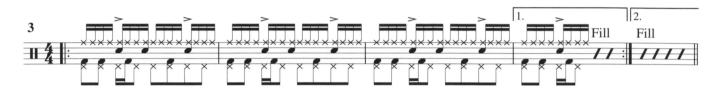

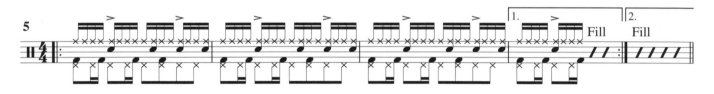

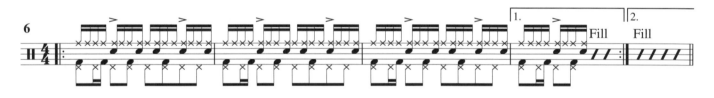

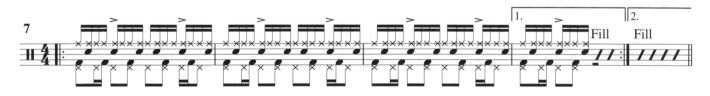

FILLS ON THE CLAVE

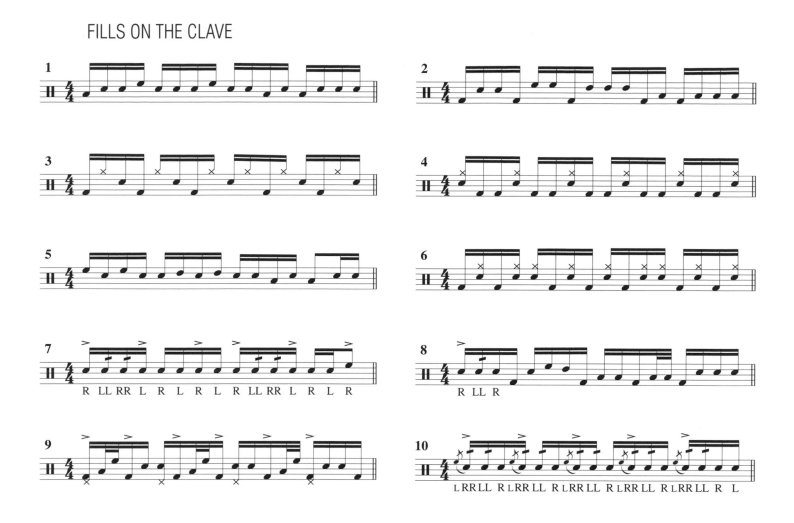

Worksheet

Keep the ideas flowing. These are only my ideas on the clave pattern—no telling what you'll come up with.

AFRO CUBAN FILLS

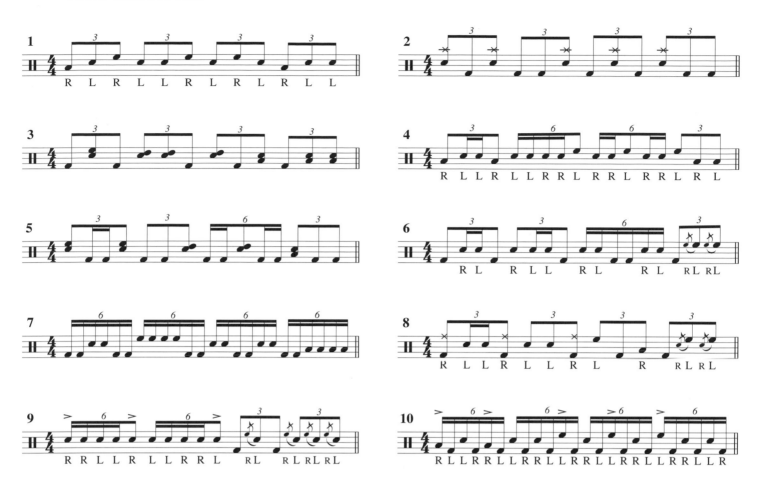

Worksheet

By now, you've gone through all of the clave patterns. Write down some of your favorite grooves and fills. This can really help you remember.

SPLASHING THE HI-HAT

Start with your heel up. Lower your heel onto the foot board, raise the front part of your foot, and let the hi-hat open up slightly. Close the hi-hat with the ball of your foot and return to the starting position with your heel up. This is a cool technique. It adds fullness to the grooves while playing the ride or hi-hat.

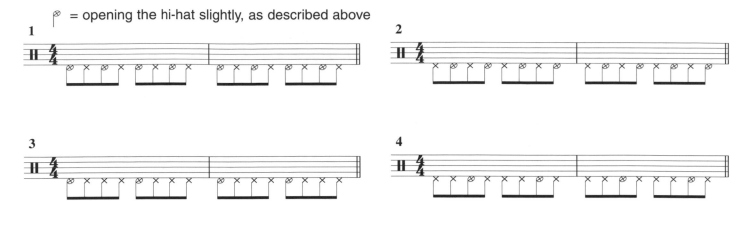

CLAVE GROOVES WITH SPLASHING THE HI-HAT

VARIOUS CLAVE GROOVES WITH SPLASHING ON THE HI-HAT

Worksheet

Play your favorite clave pattern on the bass drum while splashing the hi-hat on the quarters, and orchestrate various clave patterns on the drums. Think in four- and eight-bar phrases.

QUICK REFERENCE GUIDE

Here's a quick reference guide to all of the clave grooves and the accent patterns to create fills.

Worksheet

Try your hand at writing your own grooves and orchestrating your own fills.

Chapter 4:
PLAYING THE CHARTS

Now it's time to put it all together. Listen to the first track with the drums to get the idea. Then play along with the track that does not include the drums. Remember when playing the groove to pay attention to the dynamics with respect to ghost notes. Make sure the backbeat and ghost notes have dynamic contrast.

For the fills, think in clave and use the five methods to construct and create fills.

Each time you play the track, use different fills. When playing the groove, vary the bass drum pattern as well.

For example:

Also, when playing the ride, combine different ostinatos to promote variety.

For example:

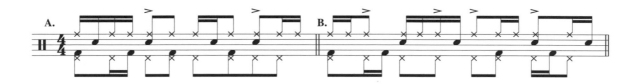

You always need a seed to make something grow, and your clave rhythm is your seed. Going through this book not only gives you great four-way coordination, but provides you with the ability to plug yourself into many different styles of music: rock, funk, hip-hop, jazz, and a variety of ethnic styles.

The variations are endless once you have this foundational technique underway.

CHART 1: BOMBO

CHART 2: SON

Track 3
with drums

Track 4
without drums

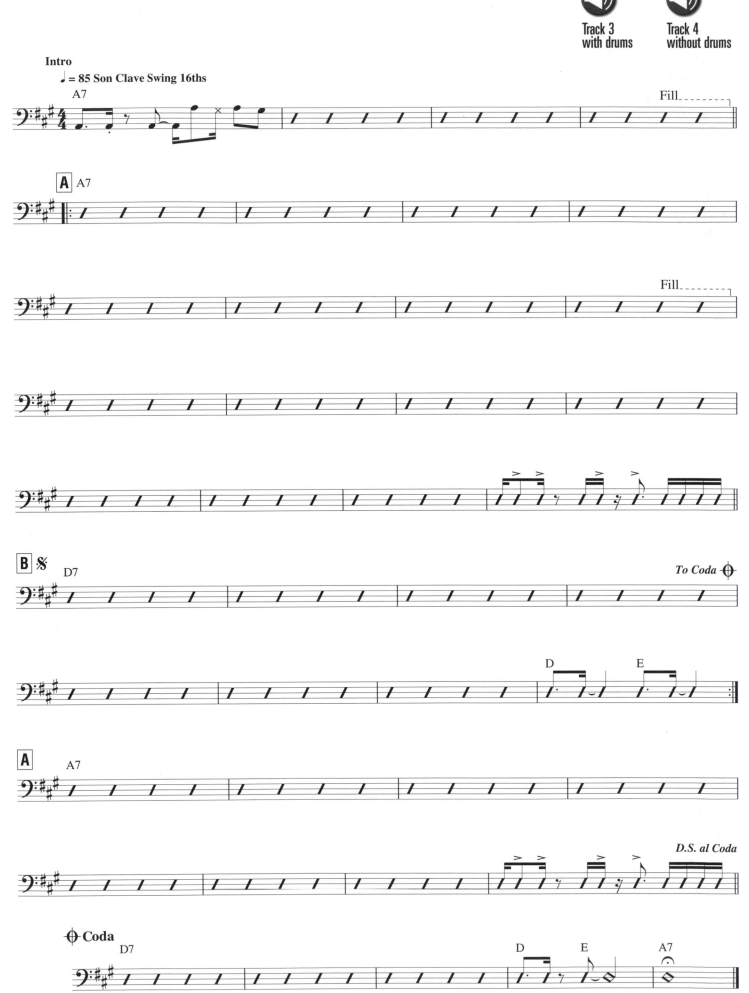

38

CHART 3: RUMBA

Track 5
with drums

Track 6
without drums

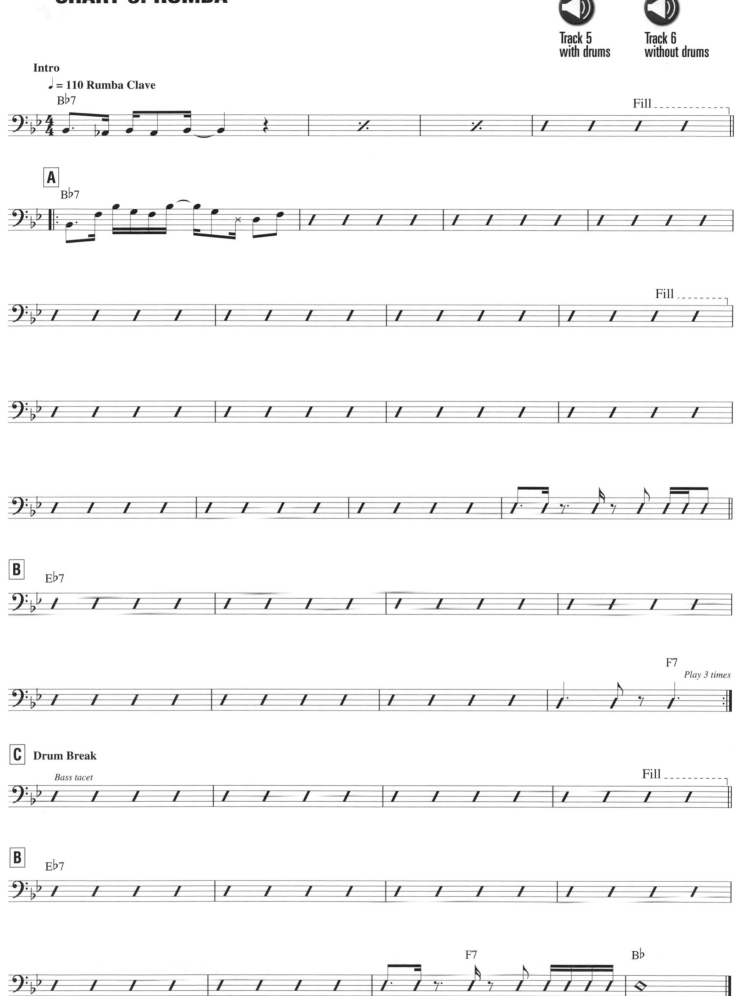

CHART 4: BOSSA

CHART 5: AFRO CUBAN

CHART 6: SAMBA

Track 11
with drums

Track 12
without drums

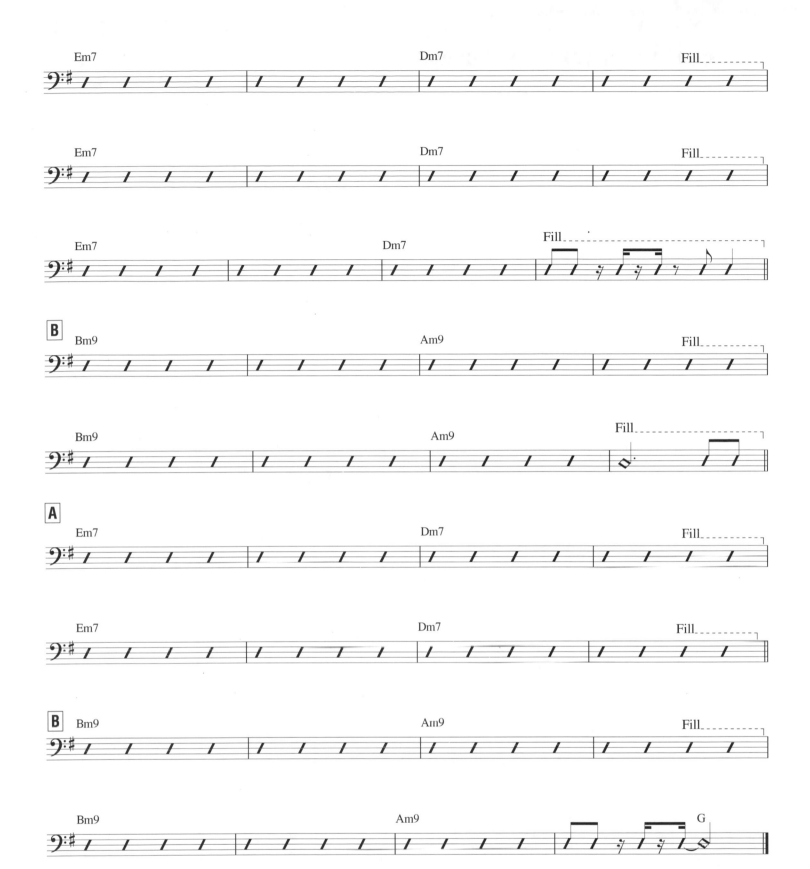

CHART 7: ALTERNATIVE CLAVE

Track 13
with drums

Track 14
without drums

CONCLUSION

In closing, I hope you've gained more awareness on how valuable the clave is as a source from which to create. I consider the claves the rudiments of creating grooves and fills. Fads come and go, but having this foundational knowledge helps you adapt to the changing times. Keep practicing and expanding your ideas. I wish you much success in whatever you pursue.

John Snider, Jr.

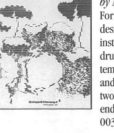

Transcribed SCORES®

00672463	Aerosmith – Big Ones	$24.95
00673228	The Beatles – Complete Scores (Boxed Set)	$79.95
00672378	The Beatles – Transcribed Scores	$24.95
00672459	George Benson Collection	$24.95
00673208	Best of Blood, Sweat & Tears	$19.95
00672503	Cheap Trick – Greatest Hits	$24.95
00672367	Chicago – Volume 1	$24.95
00672368	Chicago – Volume 2	$24.95
00672460	Miles Davis – Kind of Blue (Sketch Scores)	$19.95
00672490	Miles Davis – Kind of Blue (Hardcover)	$29.95
00672502	Deep Purple – Greatest Hits	$24.95
00672327	Gil Evans Collection	$24.95
00672508	Ben Folds – Rockin' the Suburbs	$19.95
00672427	Ben Folds Five – Selections from Naked Baby Photos	$19.95
00672458	Ben Folds Five – The Unauthorized Biography of Reinhold Messner	$19.95
00672428	Ben Folds Five – Whatever and Ever, Amen	$19.95
00672399	Foo Fighters	$24.95
00672442	Foo Fighters – The Colour and the Shape	$24.95
00672517	Foo Fighters – One by One	$24.95
00672477	Foo Fighters – There Is Nothing Left to Lose	$24.95
00672472	Goo Goo Dolls Collection	$24.95
00672308	Jimi Hendrix – Are You Experienced?	$29.95
00672345	Jimi Hendrix – Axis Bold As Love	$29.95
00672313	Jimi Hendrix – Band of Gypsys	$29.95
00672311	Jimi Hendrix – Electric Ladyland	$29.95
00672397	Jimi Hendrix – Experience Hendrix	$29.95
00672500	Best of Incubus	$24.95
00672469	Billy Joel Collection	$24.95
00672415	Eric Johnson – Ah Via Musicom	$24.95
00672470	Carole King – Greatest Hits	$24.95
00672499	John Lennon – Greatest Hits	$24.95
00672465	John Lennon – Imagine	$24.95

00672478	The Best of Megadeth	$24.95
00672409	Megadeth – Rust in Peace	$24.95
00672504	Gary Moore – Greatest Hits	$24.95
00690582	Nickel Creek – Nickel Creek	$19.95
00690586	Nickel Creek – This Side	$19.95
00672518	Nirvana	$24.95
00672424	Nirvana – Bleach	$24.95
00672403	Nirvana – In Utero	$24.95
00672404	Nirvana – Incesticide	$24.95
00672402	Nirvana – Nevermind	$24.95
00672405	Nirvana – Unplugged in New York	$24.95
00672466	The Offspring – Americana	$24.95
00672501	The Police – Greatest Hits	$24.95
00672538	The Best of Queen	$24.95
00672400	Red Hot Chili Peppers – Blood Sugar Sex Magik	$24.95
00672515	Red Hot Chili Peppers – By the Way	$24.95
00672456	Red Hot Chili Peppers – Californication	$24.95
00672536	Red Hot Chili Peppers – Greatest Hits	$24.95
00672422	Red Hot Chili Peppers – Mother's Milk	$24.95
00672358	Red Hot Chili Peppers – One Hot Minute	$27.95
00672408	Rolling Stones – Exile on Main Street	$24.95
00672360	Santana's Greatest Hits	$26.95
00672522	The Best of Slipknot	$24.95
00675170	The Best of Spyro Gyra	$18.95
00672468	Sting – Fields of Gold	$24.95
00674655	Sting – Nothing Like the Sun	$19.95
00673230	Sting – Ten Summoner's Tales	$19.95
00672521	Best of SUM 41	$24.95
00675520	Best of Weather Report	$18.95
00675800	Yellow Jackets – Four Corners	$18.95

Prices and availability subject to change

FOR MORE INFORMATION, SEE YOUR LOCAL MUSIC DEALER, OR WRITE TO:

HAL•LEONARD® CORPORATION
7777 W. BLUEMOUND RD. P.O. BOX 13819 MILWAUKEE, WI 53213

Visit Hal Leonard online at **www.halleonard.com**

0205